True Confessions

1965 to Now

by

John Z. Guzlowski

DARKHOUSE
BOOKS

Praise for John Z. Guzlowski's work

For ***Language of Mules***:

"Exceptional…even astonished me…reveals an enormous ability for grasping reality."

— *Nobel Poet Laureate Czeslaw Milosz*

For ***Echoes of Tattered Tongues: Memory Unfolded***:

"Gut-wrenching narrative lyric poems."

— *Publishers Weekly*

"John Guzlowski's rugged poems rise like a land-bridge emerging from would-be oblivion to connect continents, generations, and a deeply felt personal present with the tragic, implacable history of the twentieth century."

— *Stuart Dybek, award-winning MacArthur Fellow and poet, author of Ecstatic Cahoots: Fifty Short Stories*

"Devastating, one-of-a-kind collection."

— *Foreword Reviews*

Praise for John Z. Guzlowski's work

For ***Echoes of Tattered Tongues: Memory Unfolded***:

"Taut...beautifully realized."
— *World Literature Today*

"Powerful...Deserves attention and high regard. To read these poems is to lift the lid on history and risk a step inside. One not only suffers the furnace but also endures, like the poet himself, the human will to counter history's inferno with an awful fire all its own. The poet's spare voice sings as austerely as his parents' trunk cobbled of Buchenwald wallboards. These poems do not flinch even as they take and give a punch: each note the pitch of absence given body, each silence a terrible waiting answered by singed arrival."
— *Kevin Stein, Poet Laureate of Illinois*

For ***Lightning and Ashes***:

"Remarkable blend of academic scrutiny with stark, uncompromising humanity. What I find fascinating is Guzlowski's ability to always say something new...balancing overarching social commentary with the smallest, heart-wrenching details."
— *Michael Meyerhofer, Atticus Review*

True Confessions

Editing and Cover Design by Shelley Valdez

ISBN 978-1-945467-17-2
Published March 2019
Published in the United States of America

Darkhouse Books
160 J Street, #2223
Niles, California 9453

TRUE CONFESSIONS—1965 to Now

Table of Contents

Forward - What I Write About	*6*
Prologue	*7*
1960s	*9*
1970s	*37*
1980s	*47*
1990s	*63*
2000s	*89*
Now	*111*
Epilogue	*146*
Acknowledgements	*147*

Foreword
What I Write About

I write about snow and sparrows, the world in the morning, the world at night, the friends who are still here and wondering where I've gone to, and the friends who are waiting in their graves for my memories to give them some breath.

I write about God and aging, my wife and my family, the way a door closes and the way a door waits to be opened.

I write a little about my mom and dad, the lives they had after they left the concentration camps.

I write about standing at a bus stop in Chicago in the pearly gray rain waiting for a passing crucifixion just the way I did when I was a kid 50 years ago.

John G.

December, 2018

Prologue
Refugee Camp, 1951

I stood in the white swirling snow
and stretched out both my hands
to catch the falling flakes, and I saw
a purple light coming all at once
from nowhere and everywhere.

There was beauty in it, and magic too.
I was a kid and couldn't have thought that
but that was the way it felt. It felt
like the whole world was waiting
on my pleasure, like God Himself
was staring down from Heaven,
elbows spread across a giant windowsill.

He was smiling at me playing
in the snow, and maybe it was God's smile
that showered a purple light
across the dark, snow-crusted world.

1960s

Living in Chicago, I took acid 3 times, cocaine twice, pot about 3 times a week for 6 years, vodka, beer, or tequila just about every day.

I smoked too. A pack a day. A pack was about 25 cents when I started. Sometimes when I ran out of cigarettes I smoked a pipe.

I also drank about 10 cups of coffee a day. In the morning and in the evening and at 3 in the morning.

I don't think I ever slept. Maybe once or twice. I remember one time being awake for 3 days and waking up hungover behind a gas station in Moline, Illinois.

But most of the time I didn't sleep. At night I lay in bed, drunk and stoned and coffeed up, listening to the Doors.

Sometimes there was a girl with me. Stoned or sober. It didn't matter.

Either way, Jim Morrison would be singing.

"This is the end, my friend. This is the end."

I believed it and didn't care.

It Must Have Been Spring

Because what I remember most
Are the colors—there was nothing
Secondhand about them. The blue
Of the sky pulling me in,
Drowning my eyes in waves.

The green of the trees—a green
As thick as blood, as close
As something inside you, your heart
Your liver or your lungs. The gray
Of the city something dry, waiting

For the flood or a visit from God—
And I stood on the corner waiting
For the bus that would take me
To a woman whose mouth and breasts
Threaded through my dreams like veins.

38 Easy Steps to Carlyle's Everlasting Yea

After living with Rod Mckuen in the horse-filled
    streets of Sandusky
I arose and sang naked
And danced naked
And visited my mother naked
And was nervous and tragic and plugged in

And I paid the waiter in kisses
And paid the beggar in silver
And embraced the silent and screamed for them
And grabbed watches and asked them for directions
And was a carpenter and redeemed all the sins of the
    University of Illinois
And looked for Walt Whitman beneath the concrete
    in the street
And put my thumbs in my ears and asked somebody
    to dance the bossa nova
    and heard him or her say
    Sorry I left my carrots at home
And I ate/wrote/cried/fucked/drank/smoked/laughed,
    and kept holy the Lord's Day all in the same breath
And rode in subways, whistling at every stop
    for no reason whatsoever
And strolled along Michigan Avenue with my arms around
    my comrade, the sky

And I was a blue angelic tricycle
And any martyr's unused coffin
And I was you or me—it didn't matter which
And I wrote poems like Pablo Neruda did
And threw them into the street/into the wind

And I was Christ waiting at the bus stop
    for a passing crucifixion
    and not having enough exact change to mount the cross
And I was a mail-order clerk at Sears who sent free TV sets
    to all the charity wards at Cook County Hospital

And I freed the masses and freed myself from the masses
And marched on Moscow, searching with
    burnt-out eyes for Zhivago
And was afoot with my vision and afoot with your vision
And was underfoot and underground

And I sold magic sparrows at the Maxwell Street
    Flea market
And carried flowers to the poets' corner and
    watered them with enormous Byronic tears
And wandered through midday downtown Chicago
    humming "the St. Louis blues"
And I wore my best strawberry hat all night long
And knew the meaning of nothing
And guessed the meaning of everything
And was a mind-blistered astronaut with
    nothing to say to the sun but
    Honey I'm yours.

There is No Future Tense in Rock-n-Roll

Jesus in the blender
Icebox on fire
Woman cracking smack
Can't get no higher

Ceiling is believing
Acid is the farm
Squeeze some toothpaste, baby,
Can't do no harm

And when worms start coming
Don't give it a rest—
There's a 727
Humping north-by-northwest

So catch that baby,
That knowing dove,
And fly it like the moon
Chunking on a loving spoon

'Cause somewhere in the arctic
You'll know what I know
When the bleeding winds
Of Memphis hit fifty below

And the concrete turns to concrete
And the rivers run dry
And the good devil man
Comes falling from the sky

Rocking like a rolling
And rolling like a rock
He'll play Baby Jesus
And shout you full of smack

Wind up your arteries
Wise up you veins
Never know what happens
Or who or what remains

Then Jesus gone to Memphis
Know that for sure
And nothing left of Guzzy
Nothing but the cure.

Midnight

Somewhere there is
A short lyric by Emily
Dickinson that begins
With that long dark word

"Midnight" and ends
With these two quiet lines:
"The train passes oh so slowly
But the grief will never end."

When I first read this I was
Just eighteen, a student.
Too young to know what
Really feeds us. I laughed

And said to my friend Mike
Rychlewski, "And they call
This oatmeal poetry? They
Should feed it to the cows."

Wishing

It was easier
for me
when I waited
by the subway
all those mornings

dreaming
of the wishes
waiting
in my pockets
like pieces
of candy
all sour
and yummy
wrapped in
their own plastic
of dreams

waiting like you
waiting for me
and those dreams
that never
were about
shopping or buying
or looking or
dreaming
of the world
that waits
around every
corner

Nothing Works the Crowd Like Seeing a Good Man Drown

(for Jack Kerouac, Bill Anderson, and the lost hoboes of the American night)

Well, the bible tells the truth
Sure as devils are deceivers
Nothing's worse than Frisco
When you got that lonesome fever

But Kerouac didn't get it
And he just couldn't guess
'Cause—had he known, honey—
He wouldn't been in that mess

Would've known when there's nowhere
And nothing else to hide
Then the dread-beyond-terror come
And pierce you in the side

And leave you hanging fire
And your veins speaking French
Till the man comes with honey
And lets the bees do the rest

But Jack went to Mexico
Went down on fire
Whirling in the wind
Like a natural desire

Looking for the sob
And the fat pillow breast
Somewhere beyond tomorrow
Maybe somewhere out west

If what he learned in Frisco
Didn't teach him enough
He should've remembered Dante
And not bothered with that stuff

He knew what devil told Jack
Just like he knew how to dress
Though just a lonesome drifter
Doomed like all the rest

Dante knew, nothing is a woman
Nothing is spare change
Nothing tells the sinner
That flesh is just the same

Like dying is December
And rocking is for real
Before the Good Lord takes you
He'll take you for a meal

And when the meal is over
And when the blues is sung
You'll know nothing about nothing
And your heart'll be wrung

So grease down to it
And listen to the wheel
The scrapping crack of asphalt
As you grip it with your heel

And when need comes to take you
And she's talking so plain
Tell her nothing works the crowd
Like seeing a good man's pain

Talking Drunk to a Drunk Woman I Don't Know

The party's in another room
but the hallway is safe for silence
and she tells me there is something in winters
that keeps them coming back again and again
and I laugh because I think she said sinners

so again I ask where she comes from
and she tells me there are moons
that never see sunlight, books that never
see rain, and I try to shake my head clear

but it doesn't help because she starts again:
telling me about the windows in the attic
the basement in her dreams, the cost
of friction when friction means dreaming

I try to stand to go to the bathroom
but she pulls me down into a puddle of bones
and finally I know her words make sense.

Ten Things I See from the Division Street Bus, 1967

1. The young man in a white T-shirt
and black slacks puts his right hand
into his pocket and stands on the corner
of Division and California.

His left hand holds a paper shopping bag
from the A & P. He looks down Division
as if waiting for someone,
and she's late.

2. A poor man with a necklace of plastic
baby dolls, every one of them as naked
as Baby Jesus, dances in front of the bank.
He is singing that "every time it rains
it rains pennies from heaven."

I love these songs sung by men with no wives,
no homes, no dinners of southern-fried steak
and mashed potatoes, no dreams of anything
but this gray sidewalk and a foolish dancing step.

Songs like this will let a woman in a blue scarf
with yellow flowers know that he too is someone
without hope or dreams. This song will urge her
to take him home and sit him down at a table
that smells like some Sunday afternoon dinner
he will always remember, even in the moments
before he dies, no matter how he dies or where.

3. And with him dances his chicken. A beat
red rooster he found in Humboldt Park
in the bushes at the southeast entrance
to the park next to the statue called Home,

a statue of a father kneeling to embrace
his daughter, his lunch pail chiseled like him
from rock that will last as long as fathers
come home and their children wait for them.

4. The bus speeds up, traveling eastward,
toward the lake it never reaches
because the route bends south on State Street.

5. A seventeen- or eighteen-year old girl
walks past Pierce's Deli. In her heart, she carries
a secret she fears will make the boy she loves
angry. If she could find some way to tell him
that wouldn't hurt him, she'd say a rosary
to the Blessed Virgin this Sunday after mass.

6. There's my pal Polack Joe going into the bar
next to the New Strand Movie Theater.
Ten years ago, I would have said
he's looking for his father Dulek, a drunk
who survived the killing on Monte Cassino
so he could drink too much and run naked
like a crazy man in the streets beating Joe
with a belt he bought for Christmas.
So long, Joe.

7. A school girl in a plaid-green skirt circles
around and around her little brother,
her arms spread wider than she'll ever be,
wider than her mother's love, and wider
than the white-checkered table in their kitchen.

She's going faster and making a roaring
noise like wind in the winter pines,
and her brother shouts, "Danusha, please stop,
you're making me dizzy and I'll fall!"

8. A man stands waiting for the bus.
As it angles toward the corner,
the driver sees he has no eyes,

not even dark glasses or an old rag
to protect the passengers from this sight,
just the empty mouths of his sockets,

red like the chicken I saw dancing
with the singing poor man. The doors open
and the blind man gets on. His feet

are sure, so is his hand grasping the rail.
He drops a quarter in the coin box,
and asks the driver to call out Ashland.

The driver looks square in his eyes
and says, Mister, you ought to put
something over your eyes.

9. Two well-dressed men shake hands
in front of the Russian-Turkish Bath.
The younger man smiles and says
something quickly, the older man laughs

and we can all hear it in the bus,
even with the traffic that grinds
toward Milwaukee with its Polacks,
Jews, Puerto Ricans, Austrians

Mexicans, Italians, Ukrainians,
even farm boys and their wives and children
from someplace in Mississippi
where the levee broke ten years ago

and cursed the family to a life
of geographical evolution,
toward this city and the shopping
they'll all be doing on Milwaukee.

10. At the dreaming center of Chicago
is an island formed by the intersection
of Milwaukee, Division, and Ashland.

Once, Indians stripped the skins off buffaloes
here, and lived in huts kids have been taught
to call hogans. The driver calls the stop,
and the blind man is first to leave the bus,
thanking the driver for his courtesy.

A woman presses the blind man forward.
She's in a hurry, and he understands.
His grip is still sure on the rail, and he's
getting off as fast as he can. I'm behind him,
and I'm behind her and leave the bus in turn
walking quickly to the subway entrance.

A legless man sitting on the sidewalk
raises his wool cap to me and in Polish
offers me a pencil. Like my mother taught me,
I toss a quarter in his cap and say in Polish,
"Thanks, but you keep the pencil. I've got plenty."

When the Moon Was in the Seventh House

I hitchhiked through the alignment of the stars,
but God never spoke to me like a son. Somewhere
in my acid dreams there was talk of ice cream,
chocolate shakes graced with Nutella,
an ice cream parlor on wheels visiting the poor
of Costa Rica and Guatemala.
Someone said I'd be the missionary of love
offering them each a spoonful of berry gelato.

Of course, I awoke and found myself
in a strange hotel in Elko, Nevada.
Searching for coffee, I walked down a hall
and found a black plastic bag. Just beyond it
was a q-tip. Beyond that was a lobby
where an urn of dark roasted coffee
rested on a beautiful table. Someone had spilled
all the milk and cream, and the cups were gone.

But I knew tomorrow there would be poems
and a sky full of angels in the shape
of translucent tennis balls, and until then
we would have to work in the factory of life,
sorting the debris left by the giants of the last age,
the age of wars and railroads that brought all of us
to the ovens, even those of who weren't born yet
and never would know the voice of God and sorrow.

True Confessions: 1968 and 1969

1. The Siege of Khe Sanh

The Vietnam War wasn't much in my life.
Marching in the spring demonstrations,
I wasn't thinking of my black and white brothers
stalking through the green mazes

or shaking through the incoming rounds
exploding into killing bits of steel
around them. My thoughts were all on love,
on Nancy, the hippie girl yearning for me

and the dreams we wove in our letters
that built a bridge of love and dreams
we were sure would bring us finally
together, but that spring I couldn't wait

and I dropped out and hitched to Maryland.
I wanted to touch her, feel the weight
and shape of her breasts when she rolled
her gray sweater above her head and said,

"Don't be so shy, John, don't you love them,"
and I did, more than the dreams of beaches
and waking in a house among green
and red flowers with the scent of sunlight

stirring the curtains softly, not enough
to wake her from her dreams but enough
to wake me so I could follow the curve
of her chin and imagine the taste

of her hair in my mouth. Vanilla,
sweet apricots, and something salty,
maybe my sweat after we made love.
The dreams kept me writing, imagining

her but they weren't enough. So while
my brothers in Vietnam pressed their backs
against the sandbag shacks of Khe Sanh,
I hitched for twenty-three hours east

to Maryland. But none of it worked out
the way I'd imagined. She was still
in school, preparing a project
on the peasants of the Mekong Delta,

and drafting a final paper on *Crime*
and Punishment, asking me what
I thought Raskolnikov's final sin was.
The pride that drove him to drive his axe

into the old lady's head, or the love
he always felt for his sister and mother?
And sometimes we'd walk the lazy paths
of the campus at night, stop on a bench

and neck, or sneak into her dorm room
and press against each other, my hands
on the breasts beneath her gray sweater,
her palms rolling soft circles on my chest

but mainly I sat in a diner off campus
dreaming and spinning a silver dollar
toward a .22 cartridge shell standing
upright on the counter near an ashtray.

2. Dreaming—A Year Later

We were in my parents' kitchen,
the rooms quiet. The sunlight
in the windows in the afternoon
spinning the rooms to gold

and she said she didn't love me
that she had come from Maryland
to tell me she was seeing me
for the last time, and that my love

was not enough to keep her with me
dreaming of California
and she was moving to Frisco
and this was the end of the dream

and I went to my parents' bedroom
and pulled the gun from the drawer
and I grabbed her arm so tight
she could hardly pull away,

and I pointed the gun at her face
and said I would shoot her
and then I would shoot myself
because she didn't love me

and I didn't even know if the gun
was loaded, or if it was real
or if I was just joking
and she said she didn't love me

and that I should really do it
if I was going to do it
just right there in the kitchen
where we spent so much time

dreaming of us in California
and she said John just do it
if you're going to do it. Do it
because I don't love you and don't care

if I go to California alone
or die here with you, and I said
I would do it, really I would.
I would take the revolver

and do it. I would do it because
I couldn't live without her dreaming
with me about California
and cold beaches and red wine,

those dreams that filled our love
with all the glory and beauty,
all the time and sunlight
I ever thought we ever needed

and she said just do it, just do it,
just press the gun there and do it
and I knew I couldn't do it
in the kitchen with the sunlight

so pure almost like the sunlight
on the cold beaches in California
and I let the revolver drop
to the floor and said I can't do it.

She said it again, I don't love you,
and I couldn't look at her,
and I asked her what we'd do now,
and she shook her arm loose from mine.

Tonight the Beach is Silent

There are no swimmers here tonight
The water is cold and moon dark

A man rests for a moment on a bench
And watches the waves for no reason

A white car pulls into a parking lot
Makes a slow circle and leaves

A woman walks backward in the sand
Holding her scarf hard against her head

She may be dreaming, her eyes
Watching the imprints left by her shoes

A white plastic grocery bag balloons
Along the grass. It's going nowhere

Just moving, sometimes slowly
Sometimes fast as the wind picks up

I can hear the water, the almost quiet waves
Shoosing across the wet cold sand

No other sounds now, not cars
Not voices of young boys playing

Tag in the grass beyond the red slat
And wire storm fence leaning

Wave-like toward me and then away

Remembering

Does she still own the dress she bought that day,
The one with flowers painted thin and faded
By some street artist who charged us too much?

And where did she go? On good days I think
We're still together; on bad ones, I know
We're the dark land between us, saying nothing,
Wondering where the words are we spent
So easily that Saturday afternoon in Chicago
When she twirled and turned and twirled again.

I see those Guernseys still, their heads
Like soft hammers in that cold late April
Pressing against the fence of the farm in the zoo.

Did she say anything? Look at me a certain way?
I only remember her dress and the wind
From Lake Michigan moving through her body
Like an anaconda grown slow on discarded rinds.

The Second Time I Went Crazy

I stood on North Avenue Beach
In November, the sand frozen, hard
Solid beneath my feet like glass
Or rocks, things without give, and stared

At the dark water moving slowly without
Waves or motion, any sense of a world
Alive, and the few stars that I could see
Were swirling, pulling me toward them

Like magnets and my body did not want
To go. It wanted to fall to the sand,
Just fall there, and I fell to my knees
And dug my hands into the sand, thinking

If I could press my hands into the sand
I would be safe. The stars would not
Have me, they would not hurt me.
And I knelt there for a long time,

My eyes closed so that I could not
See the stars swirling because if I
Couldn't see them they would not pull
Me up to them, fill me with their cold

Light and their madness, none of it
Would touch me. But I knew kneeling
Was madness too, this fear of the stars,
This gripping the sand, my body drawn

In two directions for no reason
I could explain then or even now.
All of it just started as I stood
Looking at the black, still water

And the stars that began to move me
as I stared at their bright stillness,
the spirit soul in the sky trying
To punish me, or raise me to the light

Or something.

Climbing Down from the Wind

There was no history there, no biography,
just me walking into a room,
looking at the paintings framed on the wall.

The colors seemed flat, foolish, too much washed
blue, forgotten yellow. The boat in this one
too small, the cliffs in that, too distant.

There were other thoughts on my mind too:
some about Chopin, his precise touch,
his memories of exile; some about

what I saw earlier through the window:
two lovers in a red car, the girl's shoulder
a shadow over the boy's chest and neck,

his eyes graced with stubborn wonder.
It's then I become aware of the gun in my hand,
its weight, its thereness. If I could've

put it down, I would've. If I could've sung
I would've done that too, but it didn't seem
a time for singing. I knew that

as I stood, first before the TV set,
then before the blue-flowered couch.
Outside the house, I heard

some voices in a steady modulation.
What did they say? Where were they going?
Was it the wind that made them hard to hear?

1970s

For a long time I was lost, and I knew that I had to get out of Chicago, so I did.

I found a graduate school in a small town in Indiana where I didn't know where the drugs were, and I moved into a dorm and lived without coffee and too much booze.

And I read Bellow and Shakespeare and Milton and Faulkner and Dickinson and Whitman and Eliot and Pynchon all day long, and played pinball through the night.

And I kept away from girls until I met Linda.

Drinking Wine Alone

The red grape on your tongue
tastes better than any love
you've ever known

so you swirl it like you swirled
silver change in your pocket
when you were a child

on a Saturday night
full of summer dreams
of young girls

with all the world's beauty
in their green and brown eyes
waiting to see you standing

next to them waiting
for the bus to the beach
or the movies

you've dreamt of for weeks
and you know
they will talk to you

and tell you they
have waited all winter
for this summer too

So you take another sip
hoping the waiting
will come back

and fill your mouth
with a love beyond summer

beyond kisses

Linda Moves across My Body

There's something
casual about it, a hand
passing across a face,
a moment waiting
patiently for
another

Nothing we
could say or write
would capture
what this movement
means to us

We listen to our bodies
and we don't know
what they say
or what they feel

There's just this slow
movement of one
closeness across
another

The Problem with Postmodernism as a Term

Can you imagine Picasso saying,
"Oui, J'moderniste"? Or Joyce saying,
"Well, sometimes I think I'm a modernist
but other times I think that I am edging
toward Later Postmodernism"?

I'm always suspicious of people
who are ready to label themselves
because I get the feeling that they
imagine someone is making money
somewhere being a postmodernist
or a cubist, and they want to attach
themselves to that fame, glory and money.

I've known lots of artists, actors, and writers,
and except for a couple of pretentious dogs,
they're people creating without recourse
to labels. A writer friend of mine
once came to a class I was teaching on
minimalism and later modernism,
postmodernism and dirty realism.
She read a story and talked to the class,
took questions, that kind of thing. A student
asked her whether she was a minimalist.

She was insulted. All artists want
To see themselves as unique. Me too.

If I was to label myself I would be
a postmodern, postbeat, dirty realist,
later-day American existential-
transcendental minimalist with cubist and
modernist tendencies. Polish, of course.

Telling students there is such a thing
as postmodernism is like telling
a child there's such a thing as Santa Claus.
It's just a pleasant fiction developed
to make some things in life easier,

but you hope that the child eventually
realizes the fiction is a fiction.

Love Song of T. S. Eliot: A Sonnet

His new false teeth made it hard
For him to speak the French
He wanted to whisper to her,
Those lines from Baudelaire,
That always touched him so,
About the light that love creates,

So Eliot took out his teeth
And gummed his Baudelaire
Until she begged him to stop,
Her tears rolling through
Her laughter but he wouldn't.

He just kept spitting out vowels
Vibrating them with his slippery
Red gums and mulish laughter.

Dreams of Poland, Sept. 1939

Too many fears
for a summer day
I regulate my thoughts
and my breathing
regard the humidity
and dream

Somewhere my parents
are still survivors
living unhurried lives
of unhurried memories:
the unclean sweep of a bayonet
through a young girl's breast,
a body drooping over a rail fence,
the charred lips of the captain of lancers
whispering and steaming
"Where are the horses
where are the horses?"

Death in Poland
like death nowhere else—
cool, gray, breathless

Ode to Our Daughter Lillian, born April 1, 1979

Don't fear
The rain in the mountains
In the pine trees
In the air
The whining in the moonlight
The wind's home

You're born to April
To its lilacs
Its silk nights
Its trees, kind
Clairvoyant
And known

You're born to April
Born to drape
Your heart
With down

1980s—Living in Charleston, IL, Teaching English at Eastern Illinois University

Nine years of grad school, and you walk away with a PhD and a wife and a child and a U-Haul full of furniture you bought at garage sales or were given by friends who were moving on but couldn't fit another kitchen chair or dresser in the trunk.

You load your own trunk and your U-Haul then, and you drive to your first teaching job, and then you drive to another, and you find yourself close to where the prairie begins at a university you've never heard of.

You buy a house and you set up housekeeping, and you dig a garden where you raise tomatoes and zucchini in the spring and sweep the drive clean of snow in the winter, and all the time you're grading papers and telling students where the commas go and where the commas don't go.

You're doing that and you're learning to love your wife and your daughter and learning to talk to the folks you're working with who don't know about you and your years in the refugee camps and the years drinking vodka and taking too much acid and dreaming dreams you didn't stop dreaming a long time ago.

Answering My Daughter's Question about Where the Water Goes

I say, this isn't where the water goes,
a prairie land of skies and drain sewers
large enough to frame her as she
shapes her body into a star

It goes somewhere else—Toledo
perhaps or maybe Duluth, but she frowns no
and I begin again, looking
for the end of all waters

Peking I say and she says France
with a certainty that has me
believing. So I say France, and she
says no, and so we begin again.

A Birch Tree Dying in Illinois

If this were New Hampshire
and I were Robert Frost
this death would go unnoticed.

I'd measure a wall
and worry about the mail,
my wife Linda would kneel
at her planting still
placing the seed
we'll harvest later
as peas or zucchini,
my daughter would circle
a pine tree, draw up before it
and measure herself and it.

But this is Illinois
and on the lawn the birch tree
is dying. Its gray
bark reddens, deepens
toward death. The dry buds
powder between my fingers,
and a living birch is
as scarce as glory.

Promenade in the Afternoon

Sweeping the porch
in the autumn half-light
Linda needs no charm

no grace no provocative
twirl or curtsy
just a broom moving

and her eyes on the child
between the trees moving
her dolls with a voice

that may be Spanish or French
or some tongue that only
lives in hieroglyphs

just a broom moving
sometimes light
and sometimes not

shifting leaves and dust
and feathers that begin
and end in love

My Students and Their Essays

They come to me with papers
on Downs Syndrome, euthanasia,
grandfathers dying of liver cancer,
the stresses that break young people down

and turn them into suicides,
zombies, and alcoholics with no way out
but more booze and more pain

And I smooth the pages,
pat them into neat piles, and say,
"Here, here you need a comma; there
a hyphen, and don't forget to cite your sources
and correctly alphabetize the works cited."

But this isn't what I want to say.
I want to tell them the lies I want to tell myself:
Don't worry, things will get better, life
turns the corner, diligence and

discipline will save us from death.

Ashes to Dust

In the cornfields
of Coles County
stones wait
to become rocks,
and rocks wait
to become trees,
and the trees
wait for cremation

Their ashes
rising like old men
rising from beds
of ferns and ivy
slow as the get go
steady as the rain
on the first day
of carnival
in that autumn
when they first
came startled
by the angel beauty
of hands husking corn

Joe's First Deer

He didn't whisper to the deer as it hung
gutted from the rafters, promise it wine,
or sing its blood flowing into his.

His talk was quiet, particular. Working
his knife in its belly, scraping the shards
in the half-light, he asked me the name
of a film he couldn't recall, spoke of steaks
and venison stew, the weight of the shells
he used. Done at last he hosed the buck,
swept its blood into the graveled alley.

Later he said, "When I ate the liver
there was no smell, no gamy taste," just
the stiff struggle with his weight as we dragged
him through the mud and the brush to the truck.

What Reading Means to Me

Sometimes, you'll be sitting in a car
Reading a novel you've read before
Waiting for your wife or husband
To get done with the shopping

And you come to a part
About something so close
To you that you feel the writer—
Even if she's making it up—

Must have in some past life
Lived that moment you lived
In some life, lived a pain
So hard you want to take

The writer's hand and hold it
Against your own chest
And say nothing.

To a Colleague Having an Affair with a Student

It's not the sin I mind:
your eyes burning nova
as she reaches for the door,
her silver speedo evening gown
breaking across her body like
waves in moonlight,
the unavoidable hands,
the steaming
etc.

Forget the sin, it's
the substance
that has me writing.

So her daddy's rich, and her momma's
in a Westchester sort of way
but are we talking cliché, or what?
I'm sure you'll get the dowry
but is this Derrida?

Really, I expected more:
perhaps a cleaning woman
who learned patience kneeling
in the snow outside of Warsaw
digging with ungloved hands
for turnips, potatoes, or beets.

Cats in the Rafters

Among the blue trees
Shadowed by twilight
Linda presses me to the grass
With her hands and weight

But I can only think
Of her breasts,
Like screaming cats
Among the rafters

I want to press my teeth
Against their necks
Till I'm past their fur
And past their skin

Till their screams
Enter my breast
And teach my heart
To meow

Our Daughter is Outside Playing

In the quiet space of the dining room
Linda and I lay out the place settings

The forks beside the Wedgwood plates
The spoons and knives in their places.

A napkin in her hand, she pauses
And tells me again how her mother

Would starch and iron the squares of cotton
Wash the plates by hand and again by machine.

I smile, nod my head and turn to the window
See the roof next door lift, shingles

Exploding like scattered sparrows, and there
It is—the howl of the locomotive wind

And then a pounding at the glass door
And a screaming that will not stop.

On Finding a Religious Pamphlet

Returning from class
or checking the mail
I find it slipped
under my office door:
eight yellow pages,
the size of a card deck,
key passages underscored.

Believing myself
as far from sin
as faith, I'm curious.
What do you see
that I don't?

Does the chalkboard
lend my face the look
of some penitent ready
for a stigmatist rising
from the front row?

Or maybe I've got
you wrong, perhaps
you see the crucifixion
in my face, my Auschwitz eyes,
my lips thirsty, for water,
vinegar, you name it?

Is my desk Golgotha,
the chalkboard behind me
a darkening sky?

Let's talk.

Visiting A Retirement Home with My Daughter, A Brownie

The floor is clean
The uniform of the nurse
At the desk is also clean

On the wall, a sign
Reminds us all:
Today is Tuesday
The next meal is lunch

In one room, a woman
Sits in an easy chair
She has no lower jaw

In another room, a man
In red-flannel pajamas
Asks if I know Frank

In another, a barber
Takes scissors from a gray case—
His fingers are thick
And his head seems too big

There are 27 more rooms
In this wing of the nursing home

There are 3 more wings

My mother with her bad heart
And her broken English
And her memories
Of Magdeburg, Lvov
And Fallingbostol
Isn't here

Lillian and I
Look for her
In the other rooms

1990s—Still Teaching at EIU —but Living Elsewhere

You look around one day and everything seems clear and definite and at rest.

You know where you are, and you know what your job is, and you know who your friends are. You even know what your wife will say about this and that, and you know what your daughter will expect for Christmas.

You're in the middle of a journey, but you don't know it's the middle, and you don't care. You just know that everything makes sense.

And then you look around and it doesn't. You wife takes a job in a city 200 miles away, and you move with her while keeping your old job. Then she takes a job where you teach, and then a little later she takes a job 250 miles away, and your daughter meanwhile decides to go to school clear across the state of Illinois that's so far away you might as well take a train to get there.

And your mom and dad decide—even though they've been living in Chicago since 1952 when you all came over as refugees—to move from Chicago to someplace else that looks like Florida and then shifts to Arkansas, and then ends up being Arizona.

And you spend more of your time bouncing around and working on your teaching while sitting in airports and train stations worrying about their dying.

My Wife Linda Lives in Peoria, Far Away

A student comes in and I invite him
To sit, relax, and smoke a cigarette
If he's got one. It's all right with me

So long as he's comfortable. So he starts
Unwinding the long scroll of his question,
And I stop him in mid term to ask,

"Do you know what to do about a blister
That's puffed my little toe to golf-ball size
And threatens my walk, my life, you name it?"

He says, "No sir," and laughs two short puffs
Of pleasant but unconvincing smoke.
Of course, if Linda were here I wouldn't need

To bother him. She'd look at the blister
And it wouldn't matter what she'd say or do.
She could call it a walnut, laugh and reach

For the nut cracker, or if she'd prefer, say
It's like the nose of W. C. Fields and tweak it.
I'd say, "No problem, Linda, go ahead."

Advice to My Daughter, A Sonnet

Dear Lillian,

You stay up too late.

The wise and the broken
Know there are only
Two commandments:
Early to bed, Early to rise.

The world doesn't skip
To the master's tune—
It marches in lockstep
With head bent to the dirt.

Remember: The sting
Of the whip of the world
is only a flick away.

Love, dad

Lovers

1.

She dreams of suicide, a sea of blackbirds
Devouring the sun, her grandmother moving
In rags through the forest, dancing until she falls.

She knows these aren't her dreams. They belong
To someone else, a film-noir princess, drifting
Through blue rooms with a revolver in her hand.

He is a poet, older than he looks. He likes
To joke that he gets disheveled if he sees a bottle
Thirty feet away. When he reads his poems to students
It's clear he is committed to his own death.

The stale color and softness of his face mark him.

2.

They come together at a party
And talk about travel, the old walls
Of Sienna, the half-light
Like a shawl above Assisi.
They love the same poets:
Neruda with his sad poem
About a violin playing
In a darkening street,
And Richard Hugo
With his sure knowledge
Of empty spaces
And how to keep moving.

The music is loud
Yet seems far away.
Something by the Kinks,
She says. Maybe "Lola."
She can feel it in her throat

And gives him her hand,
The gray painted nails
    Like tombstones,
The fingers thin
And clean, the fingers
Of an altar boy
Who has washed them
And used them in prayer.

He tells her about his poems
The early ones with the image
Of a river running beneath a house.

She's read them.
They're a parable, she says,
Of sand and impermanence,
Wet death rushing
Like a drunken driver
Out of the night.

She knows she can't make love
To him the way she wants,
Without design or excuses,
Without reference to teaching,
Their children, the wars in Africa,
The blood that passes between them.

Even if they could
She knows she'd regret it later
Waking separately to the morning
To the birds and the light.

3.

To say something
She says, "I'm not beautiful."

He asks her if she writes.

When she nods, he says,
There are only beautiful writers.
Their faces are shaped
By the fingers of their words
And the words are always
Beautiful.

Letter from My Friend Bob Milevski

Dear John,

I'm working at Princeton now.
My son lives in Chicago with Damaris.
You remember her? We always fought,
mostly about washing dishes and sex.

I'm still wearing a black baseball cap,
and last week I think I saw Bill Anderson
on Jeopardy. Do you remember the band
I was with, the second one in Chicago,
the one with Bekka and Long Johnny Long?
Music means more to me than anything,
especially the flute, the flute is it.

Sometimes, I think we have lives that descend
and rise, fall and stumble, lurching stark
out of the dark like a reeling drunk.
Really, my only true wish is maturity.

My son Jonathan is 19—that makes me
forty-six—you're forty-six too.
I no longer miss you—I used to think
I needed to talk to you all the time
but now I don't.

Love, Robert Milevski

PS: I changed the spelling of my last name.

To Emily Dickinson in Heaven

So Emily,
tell me
what is it—
that so finally
kindly stops us—
Is it the heart
at last saying yes

to cholesterol
to blockage
in the ascending aorta?
The not wholly
chromed bumper slapping

our bones as quick
as children changing
their minds among swings
slides and jungle gyms?

Or is it the life
that passes
before our eyes
as the gas

hisses from the shower head
the knife tears,
the bear spreads
his arms,
the lover
enters the half circle
of our vision?

Let me know.
Sincerely,
John Guzlowski

Tourists in Auschwitz

It's a gray drizzly day
but still we take pictures:

Here we are by the mountain of shoes.
Here we are by the wall where they shot
    the rabbis and the priests
    and the school children
    and the trouble makers.
    Here we are by a statue of people working to death.

We walk around the grounds too
but we see no one.

Later, we will have dinner
in the cafeteria at Auschwitz.

We will eat off aluminum plates
with aluminum knives and forks.
The beans will be hard,
and the bread will be tasteless.

But for right now, we take more pictures:

Here we are by the mountain of empty suitcases.
Here we are in front of the big ovens.
Here we are by the gate with the famous slogan.
Here we are in front of the pond
    where the water is still gray from the ashes
    the Germans dumped.

At 40 My Wife Linda Begins Writing Poems

Each night, they come to her in dreams,
and when she can't listen anymore,
she wakes and writes in darkness,
the shadows from the street falling
through the blinds, and onto the paper,
like whispers.

She feels me there beside her,
sleeping in a world without dreams,
or horizons, a beached whale, all breath
and cold flesh. When she reads her poems
to me in the morning kitchen, I'm puzzled,
frightened. Don't worry, she says, I love you
more than anything.

She dreams one night she is driving
in the desert, wind moving through the air
like lean snakes. Hungry, she stops
near a gray shed. Sees the bones
of three angels lying on a table,
and urinates into a tub
filled with photos. In the corner
her mother stands in red stockings,
her feet swollen like salmon,
her tongue adrift in a dark sea,
her lips shaping sighs, maybe questions,
each one as different as blue
and yellow.

When Linda wakes, the lines are scrimshaw,
circles flattening under the weight
of triangles, gashes, red birds in trees.
I put down my coffee cup,
search her eyes. She knows
what all of it means.

Icarus

Below me, I see
the water's
muddy gray waves
but no mother
no father.

They are far
from where I am,
here in these clouds
bound to these wings
with plastic ropes
and butcher's string.

My parents are elsewhere,
beyond the mountains
in the deserts
west of Phoenix

where in the evening
they sit at the table,
my father reading
the bible, the story
of Peter hiding
in the shadows

my mother playing
with her photographs:
a mouth forced open
by death, a wedding
she no longer remembers,
a lost boy with a round ball

and parachute pants

the sun is hot and close

What the Tower of Babel Looks Like

It looks like
The stones in your hands
The ones in your eyes
The ones beside you
When you sit on the ground

It looks like the weather
When the weather
Is hard and the clouds
Press down on you
Till you think
You'll never breathe
Again

Babel is the sorrow
Mothers feel
When their daughters
Won't call them
And the years roll
And they don't call

Babel looks like
Saturday night
In a small town
On the prairie
In Illinois
After the farmers
Leave for better
Places

It looks like
Everything you never
Want to see

And someday
Will

Channel Surfing

I stop when I see Sister Xavier,
the nun I had in 6th grade,
and I wonder how she's still alive
after all these fifty-one years.

She was old then, and loved
to tell us about the first time
she saw ice-cream, how amazed
she was not by its coldness
or its sweetness but by the miracle
of its colors. She'd never seen
a white so blue, a strawberry so red.

And here she is still telling me
to get on my knees every night
like a good boy and ask Jesus
to forgive me for being bad
and pray to Him always
to help me be better tomorrow.

And I nod my head and think
maybe that's not such a bad idea.

Drought Summer

See my little girl, Lillian?
She can read a book

make change for a twenty
tell you what star is what.

She doesn't need
school or love or dolls.

She knows winter is hard
and beds are soft

pumpkins
grow on vines.

She knows
what's useless:

the soft spade
the easy turn.

Maybe in Mississippi
somewhere

the soil is wet and sweet
ready for asparagus

or juicy fruit
but not here.

Here the ground is clay
more clay than dirt.

Here, if you see a dog,
you know he's leaving.

Short Poem Written before Bedtime

The room rests already,
The books on the desk waiting
For the lights to go out, the door
To close. They are happy
That the reading is done.

Their words get so weary
When my eyes go over them
Again and again, sometimes
Like coarse sandpaper looking
To get to the beautiful wood
Beneath the layers of varnish,
Sometimes like flowers
Drifting from the hands
Of a young church girl
Who wants to make the path
Beautiful for the Blessed Virgin.

So tired now, but tomorrow
These books will be happy
to be seen.

Tomorrow.

I Listen to My Father Dying

He groans again
and it sounds
almost like the laugh
of a man in pain

a monotone,
one quick exhaled "ha"
followed by another,

the clear sound of fear
deep in his throat
and maybe deeper

He's dreaming
of something
coming after him

that will not stop
until it drags him down
and kills him

I try to wake him
with a hand on his cheek
but he won't wake.

Sometimes I Wish I had a Theory of Poetry

I read about Ryszard Krynicki's
"Linguistic poetry" and Karpowicz's
"Mallarmean" objectification
Of language and Czerniawski's
"Specific relativism" that stems
Like a branch from the tree of British
Linguistic philosophy,

And I hide my poems
With their prairie plainness,
Their beets and trains and sparrows
In shame,

And I wonder how I got
To this plain corner, this non-abstract
Joining of plain streets where my words
Are as simple as a handful of raisins
In the palm of my hand.

Wasn't I paying attention
In Sandra Bartkey's Philosophy class?
Or was my time for learning these things
In my twenties when too often
I was drunk or hungover?

And clearly it's too late now
For me to stiffen my lines
With philosophical verve. Derrida
And Foucault are as beyond me
As Bakhtin's Russian with
Its Cyrillic pagodas.

My mind gravitates
(Oh that heavy, slow word)
To pauses, and I find I like
To sit in a hard chair and stare
Out a window at the prairie
And drink green tepid tea.

Paupers' Graves, West Peoria, Illinois

Here you will learn all
you need to know about
addition and subtraction,
the long division of sorrow.

At the bottom of the hill
near the field that will be corn
in late summer, you will learn
the words that count: mother,
father, sister, brother,
son, daughter, friend.

You will see the paupers' graves,
mounds remembered
by someone with wooden crosses,
hand colored rocks, pieces
of broken green glass, plastic
flowers picked from the trash

And a birthday cake
made of wood for Patrick
who died on August 6, 1983
after only three days of life.

I Talk to the Ghost of Joyce Kilmer

Trees are never simply trees
they are ghosts, geese, and children
whispering between the epistle
and the *Gloria in excelsis Deo*
between the easy steps of the priest's
dance and the harder steps of his virtue

And these same trees are also hands
separated by inches and ages
mirroring each other in a pastiche
of *Duck Soup*, itself a pastiche
of the wars between which it was fought
wars which were like two hands
separated by inches

2000s—Good Times
(Living in Charleston, IL, Bowling Green, KY, Valdosta, GA and Danville, VA)

There are three flavors of ice cream in the freezer, and pizza for dinner. A Toyota Avalon is sitting in the garage next to the other Avalon, and we've got 3 TV sets, 3 VCRs, and 3 DVDs. Up in the study there's a computer that can do anything we want it to do except bake chicken and stir the pot, and there's another one down in the basement, sitting on a shelf, in case we need parts.

Sundays, we play tennis, and then go to dinner, one of the nice places, here or down the road in Champaign or Nashville or Jacksonville or Raleigh. Afterward—if we want—we stroll around the new mall, not buying, just looking with the sure knowledge we can pick up anything we see there, and it won't hurt much until we get the MasterCharge bill. And then it will only hurt for a minute.

But it hasn't always been this way. I know that and you do too.

The old people tell it sometimes. They start in about the bad times then: the fear of the cold, the empty pantry, the car without a nickel's worth of gas; and that's when the old folks start telling us that what we see right now is surely good and the way we live is pleasant, but maybe it won't always be that way and we'll need something hard and good within ourselves to see us through, and we best start thinking about it before another good day goes by.

Our Home in Bowling Green

At night, the shadows of leaves
and beyond them the kingdom of sorrows
and beyond them the rain and the railroad trains

boxcars from Monterey and Santiago
Vera Cruz and Guadalupe where our Lady
blesses the poor who dream of dying here in America

and off down the river the night's last train
passes with all our dreams of this perfect home
hurrying off to rest and wait among the bottom farms

For My Colleague Nancy Britten Who Died of Cancer, Sept. 2001

Just yesterday, I thought
I saw her in the classroom
Talking with her students
About absences
And reading then
Through the roll call
Pausing before a name
That was unfamiliar
A little unusual

But the student knew
Nancy wanted to say it right
And so he helped her,
And they both laughed
At the trouble she was having

I remember Nancy
was wearing a yellow hat

I liked it—the yellowness
Filled the room, a sunflower
Against the blackboard behind her

But where's she gone?

If you see her,
Tell her I loved that yellow hat

And a student was asking about her.

Sept. 18, 2001

I want to come home
And turn on the evening news
And not see bin Laden

His terrible lightning
Piercing the sky
And showering clouds

Of metal down on the streets.
I want to say to my wife Linda,
Do you think it will rain

Tomorrow? If it doesn't,
Maybe we can plant
Those red mums in the garden

To replace the verbenas
That have been struggling
All summer with the heat

The sun drying them
To brown slivers of growth
With nothing red or green about them.

And I want her to say,
If it rains let's go to the bookstore
And have a cup of Starbucks

And read some travel books
And talk about where we'll go
When Lillian comes home

For Christmas break.

Danny, Fall Semester 2001

He wasn't even one of my students
Just one of my advisees, a shy fellow
And a slow talker. When he first came in
Two semesters ago, I thought he was slow
In other ways too, but his grades
Have been strong. He's smart enough.

Today, he came to say he's been called up
With the local National Guard unit,
Boys from Mattoon, Neoga, and Tuscola,
Boys from small farms and small towns,
And he was worried about his registration
For classes next semester. Would he be able
To cancel it and get his tuition money back?

I called the registrar's office. He wasn't their first,
And I told him what they told me. You'll need
To sign some forms and cancel your housing
And check in with the cashier. He thanked me
For helping him, but I couldn't speak.
I just took his hand in mine and held it.

The Day My Mother Felt Good

Monday she'd been crying a lot
thinking she'd never walk again.

It was the Jerry Lewis Telethon
that did it to her, listening to him
talk about the kids who can't walk.
She felt he was talking about her,
My mom, just one of Jerry's kids.

She cried a lot. But then Tuesday,
the therapist got her up and walking,
up and down the corridor, twice
almost to the front door, and she felt
maybe everything would be better.

On the phone that night my mom
was happy and wanted to talk.
She'd seen a new doctor, a woman
named Winston, and she liked her.

My Mom joked about the doc's name,
saying, "Winston tastes good like
a cigarette should," like in the old ads.
And the doctor told my mother
her blood-thinning medicine was working,
and soon they'd send her for tests to see
if the clots in her legs have vanished.

So all and all, that Tuesday night
my mom was feeling pretty good.

Poem for My Friend Bob Zordani, After Finding a Photo of Him on the Internet

You look happy
in the bar photo,
cemented to your bliss
like a Charleston cowboy
who finds himself
miraculously elsewhere.

I recognize the woman
of course, Joanna Key,
but the two men
sitting with you
are strangers to me,
but good friends, I'm sure,
ones you can sit with
and not worry about slow
times and down times,
the moments that keep me
from sitting down with strangers,
even good ones or friends
for that matter.

But this is about you, Bob,
so let me just say
you really look happy
with a straw in your drink
and a friend's hand
on your shoulder.

Night Radio in America

This guy on the radio keeps yammering
about how what's wrong with America
is that Democrats have unleashed the mob
by appealing to the people to help them
politically and that this brings folks
into a dialogue with power they've no right to
because they're too dumb, as well as naive.
Plus, he says, the Democrats will steal
the next election because mailmen
are going to falsify absentee votes
and toss those signed by right-thinking folks.
Mainly Republicans.
                                        I can't believe it
and turn the dial to where a guy's talking
about the Rapture and the Last Call
and Josephus proving without a shadow
of a doubt the Millennium (the real one,
not the media commercialization
we heard about in 2000) is coming,
and it's mixed up with the Florida hand count.

Really, America, listen to yourself.

The underground used to be bebopping jazz
and Kerouac running his sloping
big Hudson down the line, and folks dreaming
about James Dean and mostly being free
of middle-class Mallism and now it's guys
bubbling sewage about weird right-wing
Apocalyptical blatherage.

And in the dark night of the prairie
between St. Louis and Mattoon, Illinois,
13-year old boys listen to this talk
and dream of being angels in the army
of some new John Brown, not James Brown,
spun like a twisting cyclone out of the night.

Super Walmart, Bowling Green, Kentucky

Three men, a woman in green,
and a child look at a plastic Bass
with a tail that keeps rhythm
while it sings, "There she was

just a walking down the street—
singing 'doo wah diddy
                    diddy dum
                              diddy do.'"

Their eyes are intent and intense
and I stop and stand with them.
It's not the song that has us struck
silent with longing. It's the fish itself,

its imagined or remembered link
to some deep and lasting body
of water that touched us so deeply
we can feel it even here

in this stupid toy in this stupid store
in this stupid song: "Doo wah diddy
                      diddy dum
          diddy doo."

To a Young Poet Who Wrote about Her Mom Baking Cookies

What were the cookies like?
Were they brown and crispy?
And what did they smell like?
And did your mom ask you for help?

And what did you see out the window?
Was there a lot of snow outside?

Did your mom laugh
when she finished the cookies?
Did she kiss you on the forehead
for helping her?

What do you think you'll remember
about the cookie baking
when you're 84?

If you find your poem then,
will you cry because you can't
remember the baking
and the poem doesn't tell you
enough about the cookies?

Grieving

Robert Frost's poem "Home Burial" moves me,
but some of my students are freaked
by the thought of the baby's coffin in the parlor,
the mom in the poem who mourns too long.

"Get over it," they say.
                                        Get over it?

On his death bed, my dad was still grieving
for his mom who died when he was five,
and I'm still grieving for him ten years
after his death. Grieving doesn't stop
like a TV drama you can turn off.

Forgive me for telling and not showing
but this pain I feel for my dad and the pain
he felt for his mom are what connects us all,
as sure as the turning of the earth.

Mercy

Some shit floats to the top
and some shit sinks to the bottom.
I usually don't wonder about this
but about what I'll be doing next
after I leave the toilet stall.

I think about the class I'll teach
or the work I'll have to do after.
I think about my mother waiting
in Sun City, Arizona, for my call
or the meal I'll have afterwards,
whether it'll be pasta or Chinese.

But this time I stare at the shit
and think about what my wife said:
"Why does some shit float to the top
and some sink to the bottom?"
And I stand right there and think.

I've been a man for 58 years
and a married one for 31,
and I've never wondered about this,
or what Linda thinks when she's alone.

Unable to Finish A Poem about Coming of Age I Leave My Office for Home

On this slow road to Kentucky
there are no Kerouacs, no
hitchhiking, duffle-bagged Allen
Ginsbergs, no mustanged Neal
Cassadys, no children who dreamed
like me of leaving Chicago

and finding Art or their fathers
or dreams of Paris that later,
thirty years later, they would try
to fashion, as Paris fashions,
a dream of coming of age,
more like a myth, that will make sense

of something they know can't make sense.
(Can you make sense of decisions
that aren't decisions? Dreams that come
to you like sparrows to a tree?)
So I'm leaving slowly for home,
leaving behind in my office

a coming of age poem
that suffers the burden of dreaming
to make sense of that dreaming,
suffers memories that won't cohere
into a myth that'll make the sense
we know can't be made into sense,

leaving my office, leaving
the poem on the darkened
computer, leaving my Paris,
leaving behind Allen, Jack, and Neal
and all those lonesome hoboes
with their myths of coming of age

that circle like Yeats's falcons
the widening gyres that won't cohere,
won't listen to our need for myth,
for some story we can tell
ourselves when all our stories end
and there's only the darkened room

and a blind man bound to his own
slow careful steps by a dementia
he cannot understand, slowly
shuffling in the corridor
and asking in an aged whisper
Mother? Mother, please?

Mother?

Valdosta, Georgia, 2005

This heart has two halves, the one where the rich
Live, where there are giant, bright supermarkets
And Starbucks coffee shops and hospitals
And movie theaters and movie star homes
Filled with flowers that stay in our eyes
And soothe whatever troubled dreams we may have,

And in the other half there are broken sidewalks
Or no sidewalks, where people walk to and from
Dark grocery stores where the shelves are empty
Or filled with rusted cans, where grandfathers
Come to us and ask if they can mow our lawns
Or wash our cars or take care of our dogs.

There's such poverty in this heart that even
Jesus would've turned away and gone elsewhere

Trees in late February (Kennesaw Mountain Battlefield, Georgia)

They are hardly worth noticing.
The air around them is gray, wet,
cold, and misty—the kind of air
you find early in the morning
in the mountains. It hits you

and you breathe it, and want more
than you can possibly get
into your lungs. But the trees—
they are like the ones you see
everywhere in February.

Thin—too tall. The leaves colorless,
a lusterless brown—fallen
and lying at the foot of the trees.
This is still winter—in the spring
maybe you'll notice the trees,

the leaves budding out, so green
and yet touched with a moist gold
—so alive, like the best living things,
full of promise, hope, youth, dreams,
energy, magic, drama, blood,
and gods. The children who see them

will be set to dreaming dreams
that will keep them alive, dreaming
until they are old and staring
at the trees and realizing they
are truly not worth noticing.

River Street Blues

In the gray shadows of morning, the blues
comes up River Street like a pack of dogs
ready to set you straight if you ain't,
set you right if you're white, the blues

comes up River like a greyhound bus,
packed with 42 tons of Gary steel—
heading for Miami or Atlanta—
that will fuck you up so bad that not all

the mothers in heaven will have enough
tears to soak the sorrow from your eyes
if you get in the way of that north bound,
south bound bus heading out of this town.

These River Street Blues know a thing or two.
They know you got to hold on, hold on to
the night as long as you can 'cause the night
is dreaming. It's a quiet bed loved flat

by dreaming, and not the kind of dreaming
that leaves you in sweat and sticky sheets
but the kind of dreaming that's hungry
for oats and black bread, food you chew

longer than you know how. Food a man wants.
Dreams a man wants. Dreams a woman wants.
Dreams only a child dreams because a child
cannot yet know the truth about dreams,

how they get mixed up and licked up
how they get spewed out and shooed out,
how they grow old and raggedy, fingered
till the colors of me and you both bleed out

and all that's left of the dreams and the child
dreaming them is the thin soup of hope
an old man living alone stores in cans
and stirs in a closet nobody ever sees.

These River Street Blues are a quiet street
of shacks built so long ago there ain't no
granny who can tell you what the door
was colored when it first took a knock.
Hear that knock? It's the River Street Blues—
coming to tell you the world needs the blues,
needs them like a baby needs candy,
like a woman needs a quick hot spring,

like a man needs the things that keep him
smiling even when the things that keep him
smiling have been gone for so damn long
that nothing is shaking but shaking.

Dying in a Blue Room in Arizona

I wait for my mother to stand
and sing about the young girl
who stares into the deep well
and dreams of her lover
whose blood gives life
to poppies on Monte Cassino

and to call me *Johnny* again
and take my hand and dance
an arm-twirling Polka the way
she did when I was six
and she could not have yet
dreamed her own dying
nor all the distances between us.

I want her to tell me
Boze Moj, Tso benje, benje,

And I want to believe
That these words are some kind
Of grace that will free her
From her dying.

At a Conference on "The Road and the City: Mobility and Stasis in the Twentieth Century"

Somebody reads a paper about Primo Levi,
The Holocaust as just another road trip:
The dying road of the cattle cars and rail lines
That led to Auschwitz, the dead city of the 20th
Century where everything we learn about freedom
Vanishes in snow and pain and gray smoke;

And he tells us Levi's death on the stairs
In Turin, his suicide's hands reaching
Like the wings of a phoenix for the sky,
Pays homage as only a great artist can
To James Joyce's dream of Dedalus's flight
Into a world beyond the poor Mick's world
Of bogs and lime and ice-forming crystals
On the graves of all those who don't seek
The road that leads to the final city we dream of.

And I turn away into silence, to my own graves,
Those of my father and mother who came
With nothing and left with nothing, watched
Their roads disappear like the smoke from the bodies
Left in the roads and on the sides of the roads
By those who drove past in armored cars and tanks
Heading for the Holy City on the Hill
Where their own graves waited for them like
Children hungry for their mother's touch
And the happy sound of their father's voice.

NOW

I buried my dad in 1997 and my mom in 2006. In 2005 I retired from teaching face to face at Eastern Illinois University and started teaching online. I retired from that in 2015 when I had accumulated enough Social Security credits.

Linda and I live near our daughter Lillian and her daughter Lucy in Lynchburg, Virginia, and Linda and I travel. And all the time I write and write some more.

And I think about everything I've done, thought, and lived since I first saw snow falling on a refugee camp in Germany.

Why Do We Age?

Is it the moon, the Sun,
the pull of Mars or Jupiter,
the movement of the great whales
as they migrate beneath the waves?

Not even Walt Whitman could tell us
although he could tell us more
about youth and living and loving
than anyone else with just a couplet.

Remember "Unscrew the locks from the doors,
Unscrew the doors themselves from their jambs"?

And what can I tell you about growing old?
That I've been to the circus and I've seen
the big top from the inside and know
that the sky of stars inside the tent is the circus?

That there are things I am giving up
as I move toward my 70th birthday:
like worrying about silence and flatulence,
the reworking of old puzzles,
the problems God sets before all of us?

That my mother loved to hold my hand
when we were walking to the park
and it broke her heart when I told her
I was too old to do that?

That my father loved to listen to me
talk to him in English even though
he didn't understand a word?

That once I sat next to a dying friend
who kept weeping and whispering something
about sand and water that didn't make sense?

That all I could do for him was sing a song
that I hoped he remembered, something
about hoping that all his rambling
had brought him love and joy?

That you can smell the human gases
coming off dead bodies: hydrogen sulfide,
methane, and cadaverine,
yes, sweet cadaverine?
And still there's always the same question:

Why do we age?

At night you cannot see the dust
Or the paint chipping.
It is all hidden behind the stars.

Keys are worthless, locks can't be
Unlocked, and still you have to walk
through the door. There is nowhere else.

You have to walk through the door.

Camping in October on the Blue Ridge

Waking cold on the stony ground,
I know the day will be perfect.
The rain last night brought winter
here to the mountains.

I woke to the temperature dropping,
but hiking will warm up the day.

The sun makes it June.
Families gather in the fields
celebrating the end of summer.

Across the way, another old man
welcomes his children and their children.

They run in the field, eat apples,
stand by the shore and dream
about the other shore across the lake.

Melon

When I see a melon on the table glinting
in the morning light, why does my heart leap up,
go out to it as it does? Why do I want
to sketch this melon, put it down in words,
or set it down in short melodic phrases?

It can never come closer to me than it is now,
at this moment when I see it before me
on the table like some small world I dreamt
as a child in my sandbox of dreams,
and seeing it as this world, I am taken by it,

possessed by it as surely as the spring
takes the elm, thawing it until the winter
is nothing in its life, until the skin
of leaves it's lost is nothing. I become
the melon's then, exist only to admire

its beauty, its lime white skin and cold sweetness,
its Bethlehem and Golgotha, exist only to admire
its otherness, and see my self apart from it,
never closer to it than I am now, never freer
than now from my own place of skulls.

An Old Man Listening to a Young Man Listening to Whitman

He spoke to me in the desert
Outside of Elko, Nevada,
Back forty-some years ago.

Maybe I was asleep
Or maybe I was dreaming.
I don't remember now.

I was lying on the hard sand,
The billion names of God shining
Above me in the darkest sky.

I was alone there. Not even
A book of poems with me,
When Whitman whispered,

"Arise and sing naked
And dance naked
And visit your mother naked

"And be funny and tragic
and plugged in, and embrace
the silent and scream for them

"And look for me beneath
the concrete streets beneath
your shoeless feet in Chicago

"And ask somebody to dance
The bossa nova and hear him or her say
Sorry I left my carrots at home

"And be a mind-blistered astronaut
With nothing to say to the sun
But—Honey I'm yours."

That's the kind of stuff
Whitman was always whispering,
On and on, stuff like that.

And I got up and searched
In my backpack for a candy bar,
Chewed 'til there was nothing left

And then I hitched up the road
Out of that silence
Back to the city I grew up in,

Its blocks of blocks of bricks
And its old people in their factories
Who went to Church and got drunk

Who hurt the ones they loved,
Who wondered who made them,
Who lived and died in due time

Who taught me the world is sand
And drifting dreams and clouds
That speak no English.

The Death of Herbert Marcuse a eulogy for the self in 13 parts

1.
The world continues in flames
swirling in the wash of his
blather.

False needs and true needs?
Good deeds and bad?
Garbage in and garbage out?

Did we really need
to listen to his reeds
in the wind?

1964 and Kennedy was dead
and the Beatles told me
to love her in the day's
hard night

But I couldn't while Marcuse
thought about his 3 wives—
the first buried a half century
before he buried himself
in Germany and then his son
unburied him and forgot him
and was reminded of him
and his need to be buried
in Germany.

The ashes at least.

2.
So let's consider the wives.

Sophie, Inge, and Erica.

Three of them.
Consecutive.
Monogamous.

Women born to
breathe birth
into his words.

A mathematician.
A specialist in European War Crimes.
A student radical who
shook Marcuse like
a "Harlem queen."

Or not.

What did they give him?

3.
Somewhere in a letter
he shares what shouldn't
be shared. His stroke
of failure in the moment
of reflection,
the pause before the pen
sets down the thought
about a false need
in a suit of brides.

His shame before their blushing.

And who's surprised?

4.
In 1964 I was living with my parents and my sister in the Polish Triangle section of Chicago, going to St. Patrick High School. Stumbling my way through in dirty socks and a white, Catholic-schoolboy shirt I was growing out of. What did I need? Celery? Carrots? Cigarettes?
I loved comic books and science fiction and how my dreams could turn me into a hero in red tights.

5.
I read Herbert Marcuse in 1969.

And learned my needs weren't my needs.

6.
My friends looked at me and saw
falseness, lies, needs repressed
and imposed, a false self
ditching at the edge
of my margins.

They gave me Marcuse
like mothers give
aspirin.

7.
And Marcuse said:

"The need for possessing, consuming,
handling and constantly renewing
the gadgets, devices, instruments,
engines, offered to and imposed upon
the people, for using these wares
even at the danger of one's own destruction,
has become a 'biological' need."

8.
But words can't change needs.

The body is the father who can't be ignored,
the child that cries in the dark till the mother
rises and goes to him now in the night
and rocks him and nurses him
till he falls asleep again in her arms.

A burden she cherishes, a child
whose needs are her dreams.

9.
*"Not every problem someone has
with his girlfriend is necessarily due
to the capitalist mode of production."*
—Herbert Marcuse

10.
His first wife, a mathematician,
ground her numbers out in a coffee mill
rubbed her sevens on her breasts
felt the weight of her surging
upward into his eyes and soul
and died of cancer

her uterus a sack of shit
filled with a pain that knew
no windows or doors

11.
And the others died too
like Ezra Pound said:

some for adventure,
some from fear of weakness,
some from fear of censure,
some for love of dying, in imagination,
learning later ...

12.
the hunger of memory.

Do I remember what
I needed?

The false needs, the true?

The love that was just
ahead at the next bus stop?

The promise of tomorrow
for the man of tomorrow,

superman on a bicycle?

And what about my friends
who pitched "One Dimensional Man"?

I don't even know if they're
dead or still breathing,
whether they need a beer
or a cigarette or a trip
to Honolulu

or a tombstone

13.
Finally, Marcuse was an urn
of ashes weighing in
at about 5 pounds.

His wife Erica
and his son mourned.

That's all you really need.

Please Talk about Me When I'm Gone

Really, I think we can't think about good
and bad poems when we think about
our life's work. You look at Whitman's Death-
bed Edition of *Leaves of Grass*—98% garbage—
Weeds of Grass—but nonetheless it's all fine.

Likewise, William Carlos Williams.
Did we really need so much of *Patterson*?
Or how about Ginsberg? Please, no more "Howls"!
Who would say such a thing? We all agree—
There it all is, and there it all should be.
Let's not quibble. Let's just include it all.

I have poems in my unpublished collection,
Idiot's Guide to John Guzlowski,
that—in all modesty—are abominations.
If Moses had read them, he would've written
a commandment against them, maybe even two.

So let's not think about being too critical.
Let's let future generations of literary critics
and readers, if there are any, sort all that out.
I mean, there must have been some real reason
Williams asked forgiveness for writing about
the icebox and eating those delicious plums.
How sweet and cold could they have been?

Autumn: Fog

In Lynchburg
we go to sleep early

Wake in the dark morning
as the birds are thinking
about doing the same.

Each day
just like the day before,
but different today.

There was a fog
so thick
even the birds
couldn't sing through it.

Death Sonnet: The Hard Way

Line 1

14 lines to talk about my mother and her death? Too many, too few. And I've never been a poet. Not really. There was that one poem I wrote in 4th grade, the one about the class I was in. It was a rip-off of some poem about trees. My poem started like this: I think that I shall never see, a class as mighty as 203.

Crap.

Line 2

The dead are dead. My mother didn't believe in heaven. When she was dying, I asked her if she wanted to have a priest come and give her her last rites. She and my dad were both Catholic, and I remembered he wanted to make sure there was a priest with him at the end. So I asked her. It was in a hospice in Sun City, Arizona, just after she had the stroke that finally killed her. She could barely talk, couldn't move her lips at all. It was like they were frozen shut.

Line 3

"No priest has ever come back from heaven to tell us what's there." That's what she said.

Line 4

She had been to hell. She'd seen her mother shot in the face over and over. Seen her sister raped and murdered. Seen her sister's baby kicked to death. She saw things most of us just see in the movies, and even then we turn away. But that was just the beginning. Her first day in hell. The first hour. She spent the next three years in a slave labor camp in Nazi Germany. She used to tell the guards that she had typhus and syphilis, so they wouldn't rape her, do to her what they did to her sister.

Line 5

She had no use for priests. Or men of any kind. They were worthless, she said. One of her favorite words. My dad was the prime example. He was short and blind in one eye. Couldn't fix a leak or mend the holes in his pants. A clown in dead man's clothes. That's the way she saw him.

Line 6

Her other favorite word was bullshit.

Line 7

I remember something about how the sonnet is divided into 4 parts, 4 lines and another 4 lines and another 4 lines and then 2 to finish it off. Each 4 lines is supposed to introduce and develop some different part of the main issue, and then the last two lines are supposed to finish it off, I mean come to some kind of conclusion, resolution. Or maybe I got it all wrong. I should Google it. Maybe it's 8 lines to state the problem and 6 to resolve it. In any case, I have to be moving toward resolution

And what's that? That my mom's dead, but there was some kind of peace at the end for her? That she found some kind of joy through her understanding that life was finally beautiful and that there were people who deserve our love and our blessing? That wherever there was someone trying to raise a family and give them the best that she could she'd be there too? That she'd be all around in the dark, everywhere, wherever people were struggling to crawl out of the hells somebody had stuck them in?

Line 8

That's bullshit. She was no Ma Joad, staring at the trinkets from the St. Louis World's Fair with a tear in her eye.

Line 9

I remember how my mom used to get letters from the one sister who survived the war and went back to Poland after she was liberated from the camps. My mom would take the letters and slip into the bedroom and close the door. She didn't want anybody seeing her weep as she read them.

Line 10

Years later, when she was dying, I asked my mom where the letters were. I told her I wanted to keep them safe for the family. She looked at me and shrugged, "I burned them. What good were they?"

Line 11

She was like that. Trampled snow in the evening.

Line 12

My sister wouldn't come see her when she was dying. The years of beatings, the broom handle stabbing for her under the bed where she was hiding, my father begging my mother to stop, my mother knocking him down to the floor and kicking him instead. My sister blamed her for the abuse and blamed me for not fighting back against our mother. I was a child then, two years younger than her, but I still feel guilty.

Line 13

In Korea, a country my mother never imagined, the living write poems for the dead, to reconcile those left behind with those who have died. My mother died 12 years ago, and I'm 70 now, and I think about death more and more. In those Korean death poems, you can't use the word "death," but you can say "setting sun" or "autumn" or "snow." The poem can be in any form, even a sonnet. At least that's what I read. They also say that after you write the poem you take it outside and burn it.

Line 14

I will burn this poem.

Eye Contact with the Dead

Don't make eye contact
with the dead in their coffins.
They've suffered long enough,
walked too long upon the earth,

smelled its sweet air in the morning,
loved the people they've loved,
loved you as much as they could,
probably more than you guessed.

Now, it's time to look away.
You don't need to see their eyes
on you as you turn,
their eyes watching as long

as they can, watching until
you turn into your own grave.

True Confessions—2018

She said it again, I don't love you,
and I couldn't look at her,
and I asked her what we'd do now,
and she shook her arm loose from mine.

What can you do after something like that?
We went out for coffee and talked,
but there was nothing to say.

She moved to Frisco, and I finished
my degree and started another.
And all the while, I was writing her letters
that didn't say anything because they couldn't,
and she ignored them, and sometimes
during spring break, I'd hitchhike to California.

I'd just stop by to see her. I wanted to see
if she had changed, if the dream we shared
had somehow pieced itself back together.

But it never did, and I met Linda,
and we got married and got jobs
and bought a home and loved each other
like I never dreamed, and we were happy.

And sometimes I still think about
the pure hippie girl and the weight
and shape of her breasts as she rolled
her gray sweater over her head,
and I remember the taste of her hair
in my mouth.Vanilla, sweet apricots,
and something salty, maybe my sweat
after we made love.

But it's different now.

I'm 70 and next year will be 71
(on June 22 if you want to send flowers
or candy), and what I've learned
is we come of age
the way the great glaciers come of age.
Slowly. One year we melt a little.
The next we freeze a little. A wind
comes from no place and shines up
our northern walls. The next year
the wind is a little stronger or weaker.
We don't change the way people in books
change. Today's hero, tomorrow's fool.

Our future—a patient grandmother
with a toddler in hand—comes slowly.

In My Dreams

There are no people,
just cars and trees and sometimes
a highway but no people.

Not my wife Linda
or my daughter Lillian
or my granddaughter Lulu,
not even my mother or father
or my sister who still
lives in Chicago.

Sometimes in my dreams
I'll be walking on a city street,
probably where I grew up,
and there will be cars
driving past me slowly,
and I'll try to see who's driving
but I can never make it out.

Not that there are people in the car,
there aren't even shadows.

The cars seem to be moving
on their own. Slowly.

I walk and see
gardens and flowers,
grass here and there,
more buildings, but no people.

Is this what hell will be like?

Jean Paul Sartre said hell
is other people. So this
may be heaven.

Empty streets.

A lonely place.

Listening to Death

We listen to the sound of death
The way we listen to the sound of the sea
To the message the waves pound against the shore
Their soft rush of foam upon the sand

And what do we hear?

We hear the things we forgot to tell the dead
The questions we forgot to ask them
The enigmatic dreams they will never explain
The useless arguments we will neither win nor lose
The misunderstandings that will never be clarified
The lies for which we forgot to ask forgiveness
The problems death defers
The unresolved quarrels with the dead

And what can we do in the face of death?

We can leave this house
And keep going
Never to return

We will not even take
The things that have meant
The most to us, our books
The plants we have nursed
The children we have raised
Punished and praised

The clothes (the dark
Blue ties, the tweed jackets
The rakish wool caps)
That make us look
More the man
More the woman
More the hero
More the young lover
Searching for love

We can leave this house
And keep going
Never to return

And what is death?

It is the hand of God
The meal prepared with love
Flowers from the pierced breast
Of the Blessed Virgin
The shore that smells of widows
Studying the foam

And should we fear death?

No, we shouldn't fear death
We should fear the loud man's coming

The pain of cancer
That does this or that
To the body

That pain that is longer than sorrow
Stronger than love

The tumor that grows like
A child who then learns
To hate you
Who will not take
The love and joy you give her

What is as difficult as death?

Nothing

Nothing

Nothing

If There is Light It Will Find You

But what if there's only darkness?

Memories scored in black ink
and scattered paper—the mother
folded into herself weeping
with a letter in her hand?

The father receiving the blows
that won't kill him, only blind him?

What then?
What then?

The violin doesn't play for everyone.
Carvaggio killed a man on a tennis court
but he was still a painter.

Dear Mom,

I dreamt I was with you again last night.

It was in the old house in Chicago, the first one I remember the number for.

You planted flowers where there had never been flowers, watered them with the water that fell from the sky.

You washed my hair with that water too. Said it would keep me young and help me grow.

Autumn came and the rain fell harder, and there was snow, and you put it in a dishpan and melted it and washed my hair with it.

You said the water from snow was as pure as the water from rain.

Years later in your last house in Arizona, the one I still remember the number for, I washed your hair with water from the sink.

There was no rain in the desert, no snow either.

You told me stories you never told me before, about your sister and the time she visited Lvov, the candy she found on the seat of the train, about your pet pig Carolina and how much you loved sitting with her in the forest and watching the leaves fall in the coolness that followed summer.

I listened and when you asked me where the water came from, I told you that I had collected it from the clouds.

The Last Day of Life on Earth

24.

A little boy asked his mother for a drink of water, and she smiled and kissed him on the forehead.

23.

In Chicago a bartender walked outside and stared at the sun for a minute. It didn't look like rain.

22.

A 14-year old girl raced her mom's Ford Mustang as fast as she could down the hot center of a two-lane blacktop heading toward a reservoir.

21.

A man named John couldn't remember what his friend Bill asked about years ago in the last moments of his life. He knew it was something about the Sierras and a trip they took when they were in college, but he couldn't remember.

20.

A truck driver pulled over to the side of the road. He had to pee, and it was another 40 miles to Davenport, Iowa.

19.

A new bride turned to the last page of the novel she was reading to see how many pages she had left. 434.

18.

The TV set went blank, and a fellow named Jim was really annoyed and reached for his remote.

17.

A priest missed the lentil soup his mother used to make. She used mushrooms that came all the way from Poland.

16.

A single guy named Fred opened up his refrigerator and wondered what his last meal would be. He didn't see any beans and wondered if it was too late to buy some.

15.

Outside of Gretna, Virginia, a part-time farmer and preacher named Charles dropped to his knees in the field and started praying. He had joy and fear in his heart.

14.

The sky in the east was starting to cloud up just like it did the day before.

13.

A writer wrote a sentence about God, and then he wrote another about the devil. Finished, he read them aloud in wonder. He had never written about either before.

12.

A marmalade-colored cat ran across the street for no apparent reason. A man sitting at his study window watched the cat and wondered why he did it.

11.

Another man repeatedly smashed the wall in his living room with a hammer. At last there was an opening wide enough and tall enough for him to pass through.

10.

The radio was on in a house where a father blindfolded his wife and two daughters and shot them before killing himself. The radio was playing an old Bruce Springsteen song, something about being on fire.

9.

The star of the most popular show on TV sat alone in her bathroom drinking a sloe gin fizz. She wished her partner was home. She wanted to make love.

8.

A woman finally sat down at the kitchen table. She had been running around for hours getting this meal ready for her husband and now it was done.

7.

In the apartment next door, the phone wouldn't stop ringing.

6.

Sheila had been stuck in traffic since lunchtime. Hungry, she wished she had something in the car, even a cracker would do. She put her thumb in her mouth and licked the salt off it.

5.

A boy named Larry played a game he loved on his iPad. His mom was yelling at his dad in the other room, and he didn't want to listen. He looked around for his ear buds.

4.

Chari sat in the bathtub. The bubbles had gone flat and the water was starting to cool, but she didn't care.

3.

Frank wondered what tomorrow would be like. He liked this life even with all the bullshit his job put him through. He couldn't imagine a better one.

2.

In the sky above Wichita, Kansas, an old man in a giant balloon drifted east toward the clouds coming toward him.

1.

THE END

Death and Poetry

Somewhere there are shadows,
My mother in a doorway, my father
Standing by a fence. You must have
Your own shadows. The dead in one
Another's arms. The black hearse.
Someone you love behind the curtains.

I remember Abbott and Costello,
Two dead comedians, joking about curtains:
It's curtains for me, curtains for you,
Then the curtains part and the killer
Appears and says, "Slowly I turn,"
But it's never slowly enough,

And suddenly you're there
With your own dead and your own
Dying, and nothing feels closer to you
Than the WOW moment when you won't
Be you but just some scattered tattered
Discombobulation of purposeless ions,

The dust that suddenly is last week's lunch
And this week's memories of everything
That will not last, and you're not laughing
Although you once did at Abbott and Costello
Or maybe it was the Three Stooges grinding
On about how slowly death comes.

Less carriage ride than bullet, it's here
and all these words are so purposeless
that it's a good thing I'm writing all this
down now because if I were to wait
until the moment of my own death
I would just wave these words away.

Epilogue

First There Are Dreams

And then there is snow
And then I'm a child again
Standing at the window

Staring at it falling
Through my dreams
And through the grayness

And the silence
Of a street in Chicago
Before anything could happen

Besides this memory of this
Snow falling, this dream falling
This day becoming that day

Becoming this day again
Where everything's changed
And nothing's changed.

Acknowledgements

38 Easy Steps to Carlyle's Everlasting Yea. *City of the Big Shoulders: An Anthology of Chicago Poetry.*

Midnight. *Emily Dickinson International Society Bulletin.*

Nothing Works the Crowd Like Seeing a Good Man Drown. *Alpha Beat Soup.*

Talking Drunk to a Drunk Woman I Don't Know. *Atticus Review.*

Ten Things I See from the Division Street Bus, 1968. *Cargo Literary.*

True Confessions. *Flash Fiction Online.*

Climbing Down from the Wind. *Drought: The Review.*

Love Song of T S Eliot. *Riddled with Arrows.*

Dreams of Poland, Sept. 1939. *Echoes of Tattered Tongues.*

Birch Tree Dying in Illinois. *This Awkward Mud: Anthology of Illinois Poetry.*

My Students and Their Essays. *Pass/Fail: 32 Stories about Teaching.*

What Reading Means to Me. *Escape into Life.*

Advice to My Daughter, a Sonnet. *North American Review.*

Acknowledgements (continued)

Lovers. *The Drunken Boat.*

To Emily Dickinson in Heaven. *Rhino 99.*

At 40 His Wife Begins Writing Poems. *Van Gogh's Ear.*

What the Tower of Babel Looks Like. *Convergence.*

Drought. *New Verse News Daily.*

My Father Dying. *Echoes of Tattered Tongues.*

Sometimes I Wish I had a Theory of Poetry. *Atlanta Review.*

Our Home in Bowling Green. *Blue Moon Rising.*

Super Walmart, Bowling Green, Kentucky. *Blue Moon Rising.*

Danny. *War, Literature, and the Arts: A Journal.*

Grieving. *Escape into Life.*

Trees in Late February. *Prime Number.*

River City Blues. *Prime Number.*

Dying in a Blue Room in Arizona. *Echoes of Tattered Tongues.*

Why Do We Age? *Atticus Review.*

Acknowledgements (continued)

Melon. *Tygodnik Powszechny.*

An Old Man Listening to a Young Man Listening to Whitman. *Beltway Poetry Quarterly.*

Herbert Marcuse is Dead—a eulogy for the self in 13 parts. *Selfhood: Varieties of Experience: an anthology for the faint of heart.*

Dead Sonnet. *James Franco Review.*

Eye Contact with the Dead. *2River.*

Listening to Death. *Main Street Rag.*

If there is Light it Will Find You. *53 Fragments Project.*

Last Day of Life on Earth. *Atticus Review.*

Death and Poetry. *Rattle.*

About This Book

The typeface in this book is 11.5 Garamond and Helvetica (for the headings). It was laid out using Adobe InDesign software and converted to PDF for uploading to the printing facility.

About Darkhouse Books

Darkhouse Books is dedicated to publishing entertaining fiction, primarily in the mystery and science fiction field. Darkhouse Books is located in Niles, California, an inadvertently-preserved, 120 year old, one-sided railtown, forty miles from San Francisco. Further information may be obtained by visiting our website at www.darkhousebooks.com.

Made in the USA
Lexington, KY
15 December 2019

58532186R00092